The Nature Nook

Short Inspirational Stories to Nurture

Michele Wittreich

The Nook Press™

The Nature Nook:
Short Inspirational Stories to Nurture

© 2025 Michele Wittreich

This book is a work of creative nonfiction. Some names and identifying details have been changed to protect privacy. The thoughts and reflections expressed are those of the author, drawn from personal experience and perspective.

Cover and interior design by Michele Wittreich using Canva. Canva elements used under license for commercial use.

Published by The Nook Press™
ISBN: 979-8-9992330-1-1
First edition, 2025
Printed in the United States of America

For permissions or inquiries:
shesreadynowcoaching@gmail.com

Published with care by The Nook Press™

© 2025 Michele Wittreich

The Nook Press™ is an independent imprint founded by Michele Wittreich, built on the belief that quiet moments, honest stories, and gentle reflections can leave a lasting imprint.

We publish soul-led works that nurture courage, presence, and soft growth... one nook story at a time.

This book was created slowly and intentionally, meant to be felt, not rushed.

To connect:
shesreadynowcoaching@gmail.com
Instagram: @shes_ready_now_coaching

How to Use This Book

This isn't a book you rush through.
It's not here to be finished, it's here to be felt.

Inside are quiet moments, real-life reflections, and gentle reminders that you're not alone in the in-between.

You can read one story at a time.
You can underline, skip around, or sit with a single sentence.
You can journal... or simply breathe.

There's no right pace. No pressure.
Just presence.

My hope?
That when you open these pages, it feels like you're right beside me, in the Nook.

And that you remember:
You're not behind.
You're blooming.

— Michele Wittreich
 Founder of She's Ready Now Coaching™ + The Nook Press™

For my husband, Chris.

You didn't just encourage me to write this book,
you unknowingly helped me find the space where it all
began.

Ten years ago, we bought our first home together.
It had a beautiful hosta garden...simple, quiet, full of life.

One morning, I poured a cup of coffee, stepped outside,
 sat down in the garden, and exhaled.

That was the moment.
That was my Nook.

My quiet place to breathe, reflect, and begin again.
Thank you for loving me through every version of myself.

This book exists because of you.

I love you.

XOXO

Welcome,
This book began quietly with morning coffee, a backyard breeze, and a small patch of nature that kept showing up when I needed stillness most.

What started as simple observations, cardinals on the fence, leaves letting go, became gentle lessons. They reminded me I wasn't behind; I was becoming.

The Nature Nook gathers those moments.
Short reflections written in real time, some born of joy, others of grief, all offered with honesty and hope.

My wish is that you move through these pages slowly.
Let them invite you, not pressure you, to breathe, to notice, and to find meaning in the quiet in-between.

This isn't a guide or a checklist.
It's a soft place to land.
A reminder that growth doesn't always look loud.

Sometimes, it looks like you, simply being.

Welcome to the Nook.
You're right on time.

With love,
Michele

Table of Contents

Part I: Pause + Pour

Reflections for when you need stillness, softness, and space to reset.

Part II: Root + Rise

Stories for when you're growing, stretching, or standing all after the storm.

Table of Contents

Part III: Gather + Ground

*For the seasons that test your trust, stretch your faith,
and remind you that you're stronger than you think.*

Part IV: Shine + Serve

For when you're ready to rise, show up, and share your
light with the world, even if your voice shakes.

Part I:

Pause + Pour

*Reflections for when you need stillness,
softness, and space to reset.*

"You don't have to rush to catch up.
You're allowed to pause
and pour back into you."

1. Rest, Refresh, Restart

Good morning from the Nook!

Everything looks so hydrated, must be all that rain from yesterday.

I love the morning after a drenching rain. The clouds drift quickly, almost running across the sky like they're late for something.

There's still a breeze caught in the trees, and as the branches shake off last night's raindrops, that cool air makes its way to the Nook. It's some of the freshest air I've ever breathed.

So I close my eyes, just for a moment. I feel the sun on my face. I catch the faint scent of blooming flowers and soaked soil.

I hear birdsong layered with breeze. I take a slow, deep breath in... and exhale. And again... inhale, exhale.

One last time...inhale...and...exhale.
That is my reset. My refresh. My restart.

2. It's OK to Rest

Good morning from the Nook!

Life has been super busy and I am extremely blessed for all of it. Every bit of busy.

But sometimes busy blurs the big picture. I move from task to task, goal to goal...grateful yes, but also tired.

I saw a post recently that said something like: *"If you're waiting for God... serve."*

It got me thinking...Am I serving enough?

There are so many ways to serve: family, friends, strangers, your community, the environment. Your list could go on and on.

And yet with a very demanding full-time job, building a brand and a packed travel schedule, sometimes I think...

Where can I find more time to serve?
Am I showing up with a full heart?
Or just showing up out of habit?

Then I look at my favorite morning spot.

This Hosta garden serves so many, until it exhausts itself.

It nourishes birds and bees.
It shelters bunnies, chipmunks, and squirrels.
It's a haven for butterflies and dragonflies.

And it gives me inspiration.

Even when the leaves wilt and brown, it's not done.

The garden returns to the soil, still serving.

And then it rests.

It returns next spring, renewed, refreshed, and ready to serve again.

So... am I serving enough?

I'll give, then rest, so I can be ready to serve where I'm needed next.

Remember to give it all you've got.
Then rest, so you can rise again.

3. Seasons For Reasons

Good morning from the Nook!

The weather is beautifully brisk this morning.

But honestly?

There's something refreshing about bundling up, grabbing a hot coffee, and sitting in the stillness waiting for a little inspiration.

Doesn't take long.

The Hostas have fallen.
The wildflowers are gone.

What was once green, vibrant, and buzzing with butterflies has quietly faded into the earth, for winter's rest.

So how can I still be inspired?

Easy. The *birds*.

They're always here. Always singing.

Whether I'm out here or not, they show up. Constant.

Some things and some people are only here for a season.

Like the flowers.
The bees.
The bursts of color that come and go.

And some things and some people are constant.

Like the birds.

Quiet harmony.
Gentle presence.
Always near.

The beauty of the seasonal...
And the grounding of the ones who stay.

I'm grateful for both.

4. Life Writes Itself

Good morning from the Nook!

Yesterday's breezy close led to a crisp new morning one that feels like fall snuck in for a quick visit.

(And if you know me, you know how much I love Fall.)

To say the Nook is full of life today would be an understatement.

The red-tailed hawk announced its presence with that unmistakable screech.

Bless them, they really are the tone-deaf soloists of the winged world.

Meanwhile, the woodpeckers are pecking at the ground like they've uncovered buried treasure.

A squirrel chased a cardinal off the lawn.

And a curious chipmunk accidentally got cornered in the Nook and ducked under a little planter.

Naturally we had a chat.
Okay, I talked. He didn't respond.

But I did ask why he stopped by and why he was leaving so soon.

Plot twist: I walked out of the Nook so he could safely escape into the Hostas. You're welcome, buddy.

Then just as I sat down and bent to pick up a pretty little tree flower...a hummingbird zoomed in for a closer look.

Like it wanted to say hello.

I let out a not-so-subtle "Ohhhh!"

Loud enough for the neighbors to hear.

Good morning, everyone!

So... how was your morning?

Life writes itself sometimes.

I'm just grateful I was in this episode.

5. The Possibilities Beneath

Good morning from the Nook!

It was cold when I stepped outside this morning,
though a touch warmer than yesterday.
And that first blast of winter air felt surprisingly
refreshing.

There are fewer birds now, but the ones that remain?

Their song is just as beautiful.
And the sky, clouds and sun mingling perfectly, reminds
me how even the smallest moments can be stunning.

The Nook is where I begin my weekends.
It's where I find inspiration, clarity, and sometimes even
answers.

It's where I reset and recharge before the week ahead
and it's where creativity tends to spark.

But now... it's winter.
Everything looks brown.
There are no flowers. No. bees. No color.

It all feels a little blah, so how, exactly, am I supposed to be inspired?

Looking around the Hosta once full and green...now faded and tucked back into the earth.

The leaves fallen and brittle

Inspirational, right? *Actually... yes.*

Because I know what this patch of ground can do.
I've seen it come alive.

What looks dry and empty today becomes a lush Hosta oasis in spring,
a place that feeds hummingbirds,
welcomes bees,
shelters bunnies,
and turns into a tiny world of color and life.

You wouldn't know it by looking at it now.

But if you look past the brown leaves and bare branches, you can see it...the possibility.

The Nook is a giver. A sharer.

And I guess I am, too.

This space was meant for me,
because I always look for the positive things.

Whether it's the beauty tucked inside the ordinary,
or the potential hiding under the quiet.

I find comfort in what others overlook.

The stillness.
The waiting.

The slow, steady promise that something beautiful is on
its way.

These are the possibilities beneath.

6. Clear Your Mind

Good morning from the Nook!

Ever have one of those weeks?
Exciting.
A little chaotic.

You have the busiest Monday of your life... until you realize it's Tuesday.

That kind of week.
That week had also marked a turning point in my career.

The company I worked for was going through one of those "reorganizing" phases.

Suddenly I was faced with a decision I never expected... the chance to choose between two incredible opportunities.

Both were aligned.
Both were exciting.

It was one of those "good problems."
Do I stay or leave?

So I went to the Nook. Because that space always had a way of quieting the noise.

To help clear my mind.
To help me reconnect to what's really important.

Even in the busiest weeks,
you have to make time to step away.

To walk into your quiet, check your mindset, and
to gain some perspective.

There's a lot we pass by on our path.

But how we see it, what we believe about it, and how
that can make all the difference.

That's what the Nook always gave me.

Grateful didn't even begin to cover how I felt.
I knew, without a doubt, that God was watching over
this gal...just like He always does.

And in that moment, I chose to slow down, listen in,
and trust that the next step would become clear.

I made the choice to leave the company.

7. Go Be AhhMAYzing

Good morning from the Nook!

It was one of those mornings where everything was
happening at once.
A light breeze.
The smell of fresh-cut grass.
A dog barking.

And somehow, through it all, the birds were still singing.

The Nook heard it all.
It's not always bunnies and sunshine.

But it's still my favorite morning spot in the world.

Because even in the middle of all the noise,
you can still find beauty.

You just have to be willing to look for it.

Life gets loud sometimes.

There will always be distractions and some of them
won't be pretty.

But if you can slow down,
be patient...
and look past what's on the surface.

You'll start to see something deeper.
You'll see potential,
in a place,
in a moment, and
even in yourself.

And the more you focus on that?

The more the noise begins to fade.

Just like the Nook,
things fall back into place with a little time,
a little patience and of course,
a good cup of coffee.

Now go be ahhhMAYzing.

8. Let Change Fall Softly

Good morning from the Nook!

My favorite season had arrived.
I loved the warm colors,
the wood-burning smells...
and yes, the tastes of fall.

Pumpkin Spice everything!!

Stepping into the Nook I could feel it
the view looked different,
the air felt different,
even the birds were singing a new song.

It was change.
The kind you don't need to announce,
because your whole body already knows.

There was a stillness in the branches,
and a hush in the air that only Fall can bring.

Chipmunks and squirrels rustled through the leaves,
almost calling out for a mate...
instinctively aware the season was shifting.

It made me pause.
Not everything needs fixing.

Some things just need noticing.

And then there were the leaves...

Bright bursts of color letting go and drifting down from
the tallest trees.

I like to imagine they change mid-air,
starting a deep earthy green,
then softening into red,
burnt orange, or
golden yellow as they swirl to the dewy grass below.

The air was crisp,
definitely light-*sweater weather*
perfect for coffee and
listening to what Fall had to say.

And what it whispered was this:
change is coming.

But change isn't always scary.

Sometimes it's beautiful,
graceful,
inviting,
exactly what we need.

It's all in how we see it.

So today, I encourage you to
look for the beauty in change,
notice the grace in it,
search for what's good in the shift.

Because, like Fall,
change can be a beautiful thing.

9. Growth Goals

Good morning from the Nook!

I stepped into my favorite morning space,
coffee in hand,
camera on standby,
cozy sweater wrapped tight.

The birds were already in full concert mode,
clearly up for hours,
staying warm with all that singing.

Goals, right?

Speaking of goals...
At work this week, we were asked to set both business
and personal ones.

And honestly?

My first thought was: *What better goal is there than just
being a good human?*

But still... it got me thinking.

So there I was, coffee in hand,
searching for a little "goal inspiration."

And of course, the Nook never disappoints.

Everything was just starting to come alive again,
the color, the energy, the quiet nourishment of Spring.

And that's when it hit me: Every year, I set one growth
goal.

Growth goals aren't just about achievement.

They're about becoming.
Stretching.
Adapting.
Rooting down where it matters.

And they don't look the same every year.

Some seasons, *you bloom big.*
Others, *you just try to stay upright.*

And both are valid.

Just like the Hosta garden...

Some years, it bursts up early.
Some years, the blooms are rich and full.
And other years, it takes its time, quiet growth, fewer leaves.

It's not just about what's planted.
It's also about the environment.

What's helping it thrive?
What's quietly limiting it?

Isn't that true for us, too?

We're in charge of our own growth, but we also get to choose what (and who) we surround ourselves with.

Who lifts you?
Who helps you stretch?

And... what might be stunting your growth?
This matters in life and work.

So be kind to yourself.
Be honest about your garden.

And above all...keep growing on purpose.

10. The Quiet Power of Showing Up

Good morning from the Nook!

This morning, I stepped outside and was immediately met by the softest little moment.

The pastel purple flowers blooming from the Hosta had not only caught my eye, but my nose, too.

Their light fragrance floated through the air.
It wasn't overwhelming,
just sweet enough to make me smile.

Honeybees were bathing in the pollen.
Hummingbirds hovered nearby,
sipping tiny drops of water that had gathered
in the flower's delicate "cup."

And I paused, all these smells reminded me,
this happened to be my Scentsy party week. I was
supporting a friend as she builds her online business.

This has nothing to do with my obsession with the
product. Right? Right!

Yes, I love Scentsy. I've used it for years.
But this wasn't about the product.
It's really about the joy we share together.

It's about connection.
About inviting people in.
About laughing over scent descriptions and finding that
one fragrance that instantly brings back a memory.

Because right now,
with all the uncertainty in the world,
connection matters more than ever.

Even if it's just through the simple joy of a good smell.

This was about more ways to support women, connect
stories, and sprinkle a little joy where it's needed.

It's about sisterhood. It's about making space for each
other, when we can, how we can.

It's about sharing the small things that make us feel seen,
comforted, and connected.

I'm just really grateful for that.
Grateful to connect.

Grateful to walk alongside you, in moments big and
small.

11. A Place To Simply Be

Good morning from the Nook!

It was the perfect autumn morning.
The kind that feels like a hug in weather form.

The air sat at a crisp 61 degrees.
The leaves were shifting shades,
blazing red, burnt orange, and golden yellow...
twirling softly down to dew-drenched grass.

I won't say "moist." I know that's a trigger word. ;)

Birds filled the sky with their morning songs,
full concert mode as the sun broke through the trees.

And here in the Nook?
That light!
That color!
That sound!
It all wrapped itself around me like a weighted blanket of
calm.

Just being able to sit here and feel gratitude for all that
surrounds me. That's the real gift of this morning.

To take in the beauty of nature.
To close my eyes and really listen to the birds singing
their little hearts out.

Hearing the soft scratch of squirrels climbing the pines.
And feeling the cool breeze blend with the warmth of
sun on my face.

It was a full sensory reset.
An invitation to pause.
To just breathe.

Autumn has a smell.
A vibe.
A feeling.
I'm fully addicted to it.

There's something about this season that invites both
nostalgia and new beginnings.

I'm thankful for this little space I call the Nook.

Surrounded by the Hosta garden, gently buzzing with
winged visitors, it's my safe place, which is...

a place to reset, to reflect, to return to myself.
a place to breathe deeply, think slowly, and write freely.
a place to simply be.

No expectation. No task list. Just presence.

And the best part? The Nook doesn't have to be mine.

You can create *your own version* anywhere peace is
allowed to speak,
maybe it's your porch,
your favorite coffee spot,
a quiet trail,
or your garden.

Wherever your soul exhales ...that's your nook.

It's wherever you feel held, inspired, and quietly okay.
So today, wherever you are...pause.

Sip slowly. Take in the beauty around you.

And let yourself just be.

Reflection Part I

This section was about slowing down, about listening in, breathing deeper, and remembering you don't have to rush to be growing.

Now that you've read these first few stories, take a few quiet moments for yourself.

No pressure. No performance. Just reflection.

- Which story or sentence stayed with you the longest?

- Where in your life are you craving a fresh start or maybe just a softer rhythm?

- What's one gentle way you can pour back into yourself this week?

Let your answers be honest. Let them unfold slowly. You don't need to "fix" anything here.

You're already becoming. This is your pause.
Your permission to pour.
Welcome back to you.

Part II:

Rooted + Rise

A quiet becoming. A deeper breath. A steadier step.

"Sometimes the most powerful growth
doesn't shout. It just keeps
showing up softly, bravely, fully."

12. It Takes Time to Bloom

Good morning from the Nook!

Spring in the Nook is my favorite.
Getting to start the day in my favorite place,
surrounded by some of my favorite things...
it never gets old.

A warm cup of coffee.
Birds singing in full four-part harmony.

And the wildflowers, even though they haven't started to
bloom yet.

As I begin sipping my coffee,
I look around and think about how truly peaceful this
spot is.

It continues to give,
never rushes,
and doesn't ask for anything in return.

There's something sacred about that.
A kind of gentle knowing that even in stillness, there's
movement.

And there I was standing there,
hopeful the wildflowers would bloom overnight.

But the Nook reminded me, some things just can't be
rushed. Not flowers. Not clarity. Not growth.

Whether you're starting:
 a new business
 a healthy lifestyle
 a garden
 a hobby
 a new relationship

It all takes time.
You plant the seeds.
You give them your attention.
You water them...consistently.

And then?   You wait.   You trust.

You keep showing up even when you don't
see anything yet.

Because blooming doesn't happen in a rush.

It happens in rhythm.
And your rhythm... *is not behind.*

13. It's In the Past

Good morning from the Nook!

I love this time of year.

Winter has passed and the mornings are warming up,
just enough for me to pull out the cozy chair,
pour a cup of coffee,
and settle back into my favorite morning view.

I'd like to think the birds are happy to see me again...
But let's be honest they can fly and sing.
They're probably always happy.

As the sun pushes its way through the clouds,
I glance around the Nook.
I remember what it looked like last season,
full of color, movement,
and the richest greens.

It was alive.
It was thriving.
It felt like me in a good season.

But this morning?

The ground is covered in fallen leaves, pine straw, and dirt.

What once felt vibrant now feels a little overgrown.
And that's the message.

Sometimes we long for what was,
the way things used to be.

The version of us who felt
more confident,
more creative,
more connected.

But you can't move forward while trying to live in a memory.

It's okay to honor the past,
to remember it,
to be shaped by it.
But don't build your life there.

I love the memories.
I carry the lessons.
But I don't live in what once was.

The past is a place to reflect, not a place to remain.

14. We Grow By Lifting Others

Good morning from the Nook!

Today's Nook-spiration is simple - support others!

Maybe that means helping a friend move.
Being a listening ear for someone in a hard season.
Showing up for their live workout class.

Buying from their small business.
Sharing their page.
Leaving a kind comment.

Supporting others is how we lift them.
It's how we build relationships.
And honestly?
It's how we grow.

Sometimes you give in ways you didn't even know you could.

You think it's small,
but to someone else,
it's everything.

A simple smile.
A heartfelt "like."
A message that says, "I see you."

We all need *support, encouragement, guidance.*
And most of all...love.

That's why I created this book.

Not just to tell stories, but to offer something solid for anyone who needed a pause, a breath, or a reminder that they're not alone.

Lifting others is in my DNA. It's who I am.
It's who I'll always be.

So I'll keep showing up here in the Nook,
not because I have it all figured out,
but because I believe in the power of showing up
for someone else.
Be the growth.
Be the change.
Be the reason someone feels hope again.

15. Reinventing You

Good morning from the Nook!

The light breeze,
paired with a birdsong symphony,
is exactly how I love to start my morning.

Coffee in hand.
Camera nearby.
A little time carved out just for me.

This space gives me so much: calm, clarity,
and quiet inspiration.

Today's focus?
A little productivity with heart.

Whether I'm pouring into a creative idea,
working behind the scenes,
or simply letting myself breathe...

This is the season I'm choosing to redefine what
growth looks like.

Because reinvention doesn't always look bold.

Sometimes, it looks like small steps, new rhythms,
and learning to see yourself again.

Lately, I've been watching more and more women
re-imagine their lives,
launching businesses,
trying new passions,
making quiet pivots that take so much courage.

Some of it is brave.
Some of it is messy.
All of it is worthy.

This isn't about going viral.
It's about getting clear.

It's about showing up differently,
with heart,
with intention,
with self-trust.

That's what soft visibility is.
Not louder.
Not more.
Just truer.

So whether you're just starting,
in the middle of figuring it out,
or building something no one else sees yet.

I want you to know...
I'm cheering for you.

Because reinvention isn't just possible,
 it's already in you.

You don't have to rush it.
You don't have to prove it.

You just have to keep going...
in your way,
in your rhythm,
with your voice.

16. Stubborn In My Goals

Good morning from the Nook!

Stepping into this space with coffee in hand and camera nearby.

The birds haven't missed a beat,
singing like nothing ever changed.

It's a slightly cool start,
but the sun, warm and promising.

The Nook looks a little different this year.
We started a small garden out in the yard...

But apparently, some very hungry deer,
or mischievous bunny have decided it's their personal buffet.

I even planted deer-unfriendly flowers.
Crazy of me to assume that would stop them.

One bunch was literally lifted out of the dirt
and dropped nearby like,
"No thanks, but thanks."

So after all my swearing
aka colorful phrases
I made a shift.

We're going container garden style this season.

Moved everything inside the Nook,
closer to the house,
and hopefully out of nibbling range.

Here's the thing,
I'm stubborn with my goals,
 but flexible with my methods.

And...walla
I'm now growing green peppers, red onions, asparagus,
zucchini, blueberries, strawberries, blackberries,
and even a few baby melons.

They're thriving.
Sun-kissed, well-watered,
and absolutely spoiled by me.

Now do you think the deer didn't notice...
the gorgeous yellow flower blooming next to the Nook?

Abso(freakin)lutely!

Gone!! &#@*

Snatched for a snack.

But here's the truth,
life will *always* put things in your path.

Things that try to distract you,
test your patience,
or nibble at your joy.

But when you're willing to adjust the how,
without letting go of the why,
you're still growing.

Sometimes the path changes.
Sometimes you do.

But the vision?
It's still yours.

17. Plant Seeds

Good morning from the Nook!

Stepping outside into the cool morning air
feels so refreshing,
especially after yesterday's scorcher.

I don't know where you are,
but here in Georgia...
it was **H.O.T.** !

And summer hasn't even officially started yet.

As I settle into my favorite spot,
coffee in hand, the birds are already at it,
a soft, beautiful melody,
complete with the occasional woodpecker on
percussion.

But the surprise of the morning?
My little avocado tree... is flourishing.

Now, I'm not expecting fruit or anything.

But I'm grateful I got curious enough
to see if I could grow something, from a simple pit.

Of course, I didn't make it grow,
the soil, sun, and water did their part.

But out of all the avocados we've eaten,
something about this one made me pause.
I didn't want to toss the pit.
I wanted to help it.

There were no guarantees.
No big expectations.
Just a little hope and care.

And now?
It's growing.
Flourishing, even.

And honestly?
That's exactly how I want to move through the world.

To help plant seeds.
To share what I know.
To give others a chance to grow, too.

Because sometimes
all it takes is one person.
who believes enough to try.

18. You're It

Good morning from the Nook!

I made my way outside,
coffee in one hand,
camera in the other...
oh, and a croissant too.

The Nook welcomed me
with all its newly grown beauty.

The sun was already warming the space.
Birds were singing what felt like familiar songs,
the kind you somehow remember,
even if you've never really heard them before.

My typical routine:
Snap a few pictures.
Settle into my favorite seat.
Take a slow sip of coffee.
And then pause.

I close my eyes.
Breathe in deeply.
Listen to the quiet hum of the morning.

And as I exhale, I gently open my eyes and ask:
"How will you inspire me today?"

The Nook never disappoints.
As I looked around something hit me,
Maybe I haven't seen **It** yet.

But...
"It" is right there.
"It" has the potential to grow.
"It" has the ability to be seen.
"It" holds the passion to flourish.

And...
"It" will take time.
"It" will require work.
"It" needs your dedication.
"It" will ask for love and support.
"It" will inspire you to keep going.

And the truth? "It" is already inside you.

Whatever your **It** is. Hold on to it. Protect it.
Nurture it.

No one else gets to define it, take it, or shrink it.
Yes, it might be scary.

Remember in the end..."It" will be worth it.

19. In Between Blooms

Good morning from the Nook!

It feels like it's been a little while
since I stepped into my favorite morning space,
coffee in one hand, camera in the other.

I think the birds noticed I've been gone, too,
because they really showed off for me.

I got some great shots of the back yard birds.

As I sat enjoying a pistachio muffin
I started scanning the Nook,
the Hosta garden,
and all the greenery around me.

And something struck me.

Not much color today.
All the Summer flowers have bloomed.

Ahhh... transition.

The Nook is in a new phase.

It's shifted,
from early growth,
to nurturing everything around it,
to full bloom...and now?

It's entering transition.

It has given what it needed to give.

And though it's still alive,
still steady,
it's also preparing for something essential:

Rest.

It needs rest.
It needs nourishment.

Not because it's broken,
but because it has earned it.

So it can return in the Spring, stronger, fuller,
maybe even a better version of itself.

And it hit me...

That's what we need, too.

We bloom.
We give.
We show up.
We pour.

But no one talks enough about the in-between.

The space after the sparkle.
The quiet before the next big thing.
The pause that feels uncomfortable
but is actually sacred.

No matter what season you're in, remember this:

Grow.
Flourish.
Pour into others.

But also...know when it's time to step back.
To restore.
To pause.
Maybe even to reinvent.

So that when your next season begins,
you can show up rooted and renewed.

20. The Seed Doesn't Doubt The Spring

Good morning from the Nook!

Normally, I'd grab my coffee and head straight outside,
greeted by the birds,
the squirrels playing tag up the pine tree,
and that soft morning stillness that always fills me up.

But today?
I'm staying in.
No sunshine, just gray skies, hot coffee,
and a longing for Spring to arrive.

I pulled back the curtains, coffee in hand,
and something in the corner of the room caught my eye:
My little avocado tree.

It's more than a plant.
It's a reminder.
A timeline.
A quiet testimony.

I planted that seed around the same time
I began helping women trust themselves again,
guiding them with comfort-first ideas,
gentle conversations,
and real-life confidence tools.

I didn't know if that seed would grow.

Or how.

Or how long it would take.

But I tossed that lone pit into a can,
added rich soil,
placed it in the light,
gave it water...
and waited.

I planted a seed,
and I chose to trust it.

That avocado tree reminds me of one simple truth:

> **If you want something to grow,
> you have to plant the seed,
> even when the plan isn't finished.**

Helping women feel seen was my seed.

- Saying yes to that first coaching moment?
  (*that was the pit*)

- Surrounding myself with encouraging, wise women?
  (*they became the soil*)

- Staying rooted in service and purpose?
  (*that was the light*)

- Showing up, softly, consistently
  (*watering that mission, one day at a time*)

Now?

That little avocado tree is growing.
And so is the mission I planted.
Whatever your seed is...plant it.

Even if it feels small.
Even if it's still Winter.

Trust it will grow.
Because the seed never doubts the Spring,
and neither should you.

21. Room On the Bush

Good morning from the Nook!

There are some beautiful roses bushes,
just outside the Nook,
tucked around the corner in the backyard.

But when I stepped outside this morning,
I couldn't believe what a difference just a few days made.

Some years, we're lucky if even one or two roses bloom.
The tall pines and lush trees nearby
often steal their sunshine.

But this year, there were eight.

Eight gorgeous roses, each one beautiful in its own way.

Some are larger.
Some are a deep, rich red.
Others are soft and pale.

Some stretch far from the stem.
Others stay tucked close to the base of the bush.

They all came from the same plant, but that doesn't mean they're meant to grow the same way.

Each rose follows its own rhythm.
Its own pace.
Its own path toward the light.

And that doesn't make one better than another.

Because when you take a step back,
all you see is beauty.

So no matter what your path looks like,
be your unique self.

No matter how someone else is blooming,
Grow at your own pace.

Even if you share the same roots,
you still get to reach for the sunlight
in your own direction.

There's room on the bush for every flower.

Now go out there,
and be the *beautiful bloom that you are.*

22. Not Just a Weed

Good morning from the Nook!

It's been a little while since I've visited the Nook.
Life gets busy ...like it does.

But this morning I grabbed my coffee,
picked up my camera,
and slipped straight into Zen mode.

Slow, deep breath in...
Exhale...Ahhhh.

This is why I love the Nook.
It's where inspiration hides in the tiniest, simplest
things, like this little bucket of succulents.

At first glance, it's not much, right?
Just a few small plants in a metal pot,
nothing headline-worthy.

But here's the thing:
*There's a big difference between **seeing** something
and truly **looking** at something.*

To *see* the bucket,
you might notice three tiny succulents... and a weed.

But to *look*
to really see,
you start to notice something else:
Opportunity.

I planted the three succulents on purpose.
I didn't plant the weed.

So how did it get there?

Maybe a breeze carried it's seed?
Maybe the rain helped it settle?
Either way, it found this little pot,
and decided to grow.

The succulents don't mind.
There's plenty of room.

And the weed?
It doesn't even know it's a weed.

It isn't trying to compete.
It's just trying to live
to grow
to reach for the light.

And honestly...
That's the message today.

There are opportunities all around you.

Even when you feel like you don't belong.
Even when someone else tries to label you.
Even when you weren't "planted" with intention.

Don't wait for a perfect garden.

Grow where you land.

Reflection Part II

This section was never about pushing.
It was about noticing.
Trusting.
Letting go of the timeline.
And allowing space to grow softer, not just stronger.

Whether you're blooming or barely budding,
deep in transition or quietly reinventing,
this part of your journey matters.

Take a deep breath.
Then take your time reflecting through these prompts:

Which story or sentence stayed with you the longest?
The one that tugged at your heart or whispered,
"That's me."

Where in your life are you craving a fresh start...
or maybe just a softer rhythm?

**What's one gentle way you can pour back into
yourself this week?**
Something small. Something sacred.
Something that feels like you.

Part III:

Gather + Ground

A season of strengthening your roots and tending what matters most.

"Not every season is about blooming.
Some are about building what lasts."

23. Don't Let Life Bite You

Good morning from the Nook!

It's giving full Spring energy in my favorite morning spot.

The birds are extra harmonious today
almost like they know we just sprung forward overnight.

Even the woodpeckers are in tune.

I've been pulling weeds and planting seeds
and loving every moment of it.

I enjoy the Nook...
and so do the mosquitoes.

Or should I say, they enjoy me.

So this year, I scattered lavender and lemongrass
throughout the garden.

A little natural protection to keep the bites at bay.
Who knew the mosquito would be my inspiration?

Well just for this story!

There are always things in life that sneak up and bite.

You don't always know when, where, or how many times.

But here's what I've learned,
if you can prepare yourself in small,
intentional ways,
the bite doesn't sting as much.

You don't need to guard your entire life.

Just plant what helps.
Place what protects.
Trust what supports you.

Even a little lavender makes a difference.

Because life will have its bites,
but you don't have to stand there swatting forever.

24. Rooting For You

Good morning from the Nook!

It's a warm start to the day,
and the birds are already celebrating
with their morning melodies.

The container garden is soaking up the sunlight
and thriving.

Truthfully, I wasn't sure if the Nook garden would grow.
But it has.

Even though we're not harvesting everything yet,
I know that with sun, water,
and a little cheering on
(okay... mostly from me),
each plant is doing its best.

And sometimes, that's enough.
Showing up.
Stretching toward the light.
Growing in your own time.

Speaking of music and morning celebration...

My better half, Chris, spent the weekend at Harmony
University in Clemson, South Carolina.

It's a gathering of men from all over the Barbershop
Harmony Society,
a weekend of learning, singing,
and pure four-part passion.

They break into sessions,
sing their hearts out,
and listen to some of the best in Barbershop perform.

Chris loves music, all kinds...
Barbershop, Broadway, and beyond.
And I love that about him.

I'll support it in every way I can.
Because just like the garden,
with a little nourishment,
some gentle encouragement,
and hydration we grow.

He's growing in his gift.
And I'll always be the one cheering the loudest.

Always.

25. Put It Under Your Pillow

Good morning from the Nook!

The moment I stepped outside,
 the air smelled like cinnamon, maybe cloves.

 One of those cozy, Autumn-ish notes
 that lets you know fall has finally settled in.

The birds are extra harmonious this morning
 and I'm not complaining.

But as I wait for a little "nook- spiration"
I noticed something:
The Nook looks different.

Lush green Hosta leaves.
Now browned and crinkled.

Blooming wildflowers and potted color.
Replaced by fallen leaves.

Same Nook. New Season.

Seasons change, which means life changes a little too.

This particular week Chris received some news that would change his career path.

His department was dissolving (#Covid), but "if" he could find another opportunity internally, he could stay.

That kind of news can knock the wind out of you.

Doubt creeps in.
Fear follows.
That's human.
So we prayed.

And I told him write down on a note card and
"Put it under your pillow."

He started applying.
Even when it felt hard.
Even when silence followed.

I reminded him to, "Put it under your pillow."
Because when something matters,
you have to name it.

Pray on it. Stay rooted. Keep showing up.

And then what happened ...

Four internal replies.
Four interviews.
And one was for the dream role he's quietly held in his
heart for years.

My heart is so full because he believed.
He trusted.
He didn't give up.

And here's the truth I hope you hold close:
Seasons change.
Leaves fall.
Plans shift.

But who you are?
Still the same person.
Still standing.
Still growing.

So write it down.
Say the prayer.

And YES... "put it under your pillow."

26. Be The Toast

Good morning from the Nook — well, almost.

It isn't quite Nook weather yet, but even from inside I can hear the birds singing, sunlight pouring through the windows.

And the word that fills my heart is simple: grateful.
Grateful to be here.
Grateful to begin another day.
Grateful to sip coffee while my sourdough finishes toasting.

Somewhere between the sips and the slices it hits me:
I'm feeling a little toast-ish myself.

Think about it: whatever you spread on toast,
butter, jam, avocado, toast is always good.

It's the toast that brings everything together.
It's the support.
The foundation.

The part that holds everything up
without trying to steal the spotlight.
That's what good bread does.

And honestly...
That's what we're called to do sometimes too.

To be steady.
To be ready.
To hold space for others to shine.

To be the one who leads with kindness,
supports with heart,
and makes room for all the flavor that life brings.

Because life will spread all kinds of things on your plate
some sweet, some bold, some unexpected.

And when it does?

Be the Toast.
Be kind.
Be steady enough to carry what matters.

27. Gather Your Nuts

Good morning from the Nook!

It's definitely a Fall morning here.
The air is crisp, clean, and refreshing.

The birds seem to be singing a little louder today,
maybe they're just trying to stay warm.

And over by the edge of the yard,
there's a squirrel feverishly digging,
trying to uncover one of its many buried treasures.

And I found myself wondering,
how many nuts should it gather?

If it gathers too few,
it might not make it through the season.

But if it gathers too many,
there might not be enough space for others.

Or worse...
others may go without.

The Nook always brings me inspiration.

And today, the squirrel was my reminder,
of all our blessings.

We are blessed.
We have our health.
We have our home.

Even when everything feels unsure,
we have each other.

And that?
That's everything!

They say crisis builds character.
But I think it reveals it.

So like the squirrel...
We'll gather what we need.

> "*Prepare wisely. Hold loosely.*
> *Stay grateful...and a little nutty.*"

28. The Strength Between Us

Good morning from the Nook!

Today's inspiration is simple...but powerful:
Support others.

Whether it's helping a friend move,
being a shoulder in a hard season
or simply being there just to cheer them on,
support matters.

(and let's be honest, who isn't walking through something?)

Support local businesses.
Buy from them.
Share their shops.
Leave kind reviews.
Recommend them to friends.

That's how we lift them.
It's how we build trust,
deepen relationships,
and grow...***together.***

When you support someone,
you don't just make a difference in their life,
you change your own, too.

You offer your time, your presence, your energy,
in ways that might feel small.

But to someone else?
It could be everything.

A simple smile.
A gentle "like."
A few kind words.

These things carry weight.
We all need it,
a little belief,
a little encouragement,
a little love in a world that moves too fast.

Think of stacking stones,
they stack,
they strengthen,
they rise because of each other.

We grow by lifting others.
We change by lifting others.

So be the growth.
Be the change.

For your community.
For a friend.
For a stranger.
For yourself.

Time moves quickly.

But showing up for others?
That leaves a mark.

And as I sit here with my coffee in hand,
I'll keep showing up.
Keep supporting others.

And trust the support I need
will find its way to me, too.

29. Plan Your Next Move

Good morning from the Nook!

The sun is shining,
the air is cool,
and the coffee is perfect.

It's been a little while since I visited my favorite morning
spot, and as the mug filled I caught myself thinking:

What could I possibly find out there that I haven't
already seen?

Oh..never underestimate the power of the Nook.

Because the moment I stepped outside, I saw her:

Small, quiet, almost magical
delicate and still
resting on a wide Calla-lily leaf.

But there was no wall nearby.
No little table for leaping.
Just one perfect leaf under morning light.

How did she get there?

Why did she choose that spot?

Then it hit me, she wasn't stuck, she was planning.

She's steadying herself.
Waiting.
Reading the breeze.
Ready to leap the moment it's time.

Because she knows she can't stay on that leaf forever,
and honestly,
why would she want to?

There's more to see, more to climb, and
more to explore than a single leaf can offer.

Trust it's coming.
And when the moment feels right...leap.
A little inspiration,
a tiny traveler,
and one large reminder:

You're not stuck.
You're steadying.
The leaf isn't the limit, it's simply the launchpad.

30. When the Sun Finds You

Good morning from the Nook!

And I'm soaking it in: slow sips, soft breeze,
and that feeling that always shows up when I give
myself the space to listen in.

Today, the Nook didn't need to say much.

It spoke through movement.
the flutter of leaves,
the hush of the wind,
the way the light shifted just so.

I noticed a wilted leaf, leaning gently toward the
earth...and right beside it,
A tiny fresh bud, just beginning to bloom.

A quiet reminder:

Some goals are done.
Some are just beginning.
And both deserve your attention.

As I sat a little longer, I looked toward the trees
and something caught my eye: the sun.

At first, it looked small. Almost hidden.
Just barely peeking through the branches.

But the more I looked, the more I realized
it wasn't the sun that was small.

It was everything in front of it,
the distractions,
the clutter,
the noise,
making it seem dim.

But, the light is still there.
Your light is still there.

But sometimes, it's hard to see when there's too
much in the way:

Comparison.
Overwhelm.
Noise from people who don't really know you.

But when all of that begins to fall away?

The same sun, your light, shines bright again.

Warm. Powerful. Steady.

That's the Nook's message today:

Your light was never missing.
It just needed space to shine.

Let that be your truth this season.
You're not behind.
You're just beneath the branches.
And the sun is still finding you.

31. Plan B With A Side Of Faith

Good morning from the Nook!

Today feels like grace.
Cooler breeze.
Gentler skies.

A brief pause before more rain rolls in.

But you know what I'm learning?
Storms pass.
Even the heavy ones.

And somehow between uncertainty and steady coffee
refills... we still show up.

Still hoping.
Still trying.
Still preparing.

Lately, I've been working on my Plan B. It's hard.
But here's the truth:
Even when the future is blurry,
even when nothing makes sense,
you're still *allowed to trust.*

You're allowed to change paths.

You're allowed to outgrow a chapter.

You're allowed to believe that something better might be waiting.

Plan B might feel like a detour...
 but what if it's the redirection you actually needed?

What if Plan B carries the peace Plan A never could?

So if you're somewhere between holding on and letting go.

You're not lost.
You're in transition.
And transitions are sacred ground.

Take the leap. Trust the shift.

And always...bring a side of faith.

32. Leap Before You Know

Good morning from the Nook!

It's one of those mornings where everything feels still.
The air is soft.
The light is golden.

And for a second, it almost feels like time has paused,
just long enough to catch your breath.

I was sipping my coffee, not even looking for a lesson,
when I noticed a small butterfly fluttering from one side
of the yard to the other.
No straight path.
No predictable rhythm.

Just motion... trust... and a little chaos.
That butterfly didn't seem to know exactly where
it was going.

But it flew anyway.
And that's when it hit me:
We don't always get clarity before we leap.

Sometimes, you leap and then clarity meets you where
you land.

There have been so many moments in my life,
quiet ones,
chaotic ones,
unsure ones, when I waited for the perfect plan, the
step-by-step, the sign in the sky.

But honestly, the real growth came when I moved before
I had it all figured out.

Before the website.
Before the offer.
Before the title.
Before anyone else understood what I was building.

It's okay to move while you're still becoming.
It's okay to show up when your voice shakes a little.
To launch before the logo is perfect.
To start talking about your dream before everyone
around you gets it.

Because your leap isn't about perfection,
it's about alignment.
So if you're waiting for permission?
This is it.

Not because it's all mapped out.
But because you're worthy... right now.

33. The Storm Passes

Good morning from the Nook!

There's a beautiful breeze this morning as I step into my favorite spot. But a storm is coming.

The sky feels heavy.
The trees sway and creak,
I love that sound.

The birds are different today.
They're not singing ,
they're communicating.

 It's like they're preparing for something.
Practicing. Alerting. Bracing.

They don't know what the storm will bring.
They don't know how strong the winds will be.

How much it might rattle their nests or soak their feathers.
But still, they prepare.

Maybe we're not so different.

We don't always know what life's storms will bring either.
We don't know how long they'll last.

How much they'll shake us.
Or how deeply they might change us.
But still... we prepare.

We prepare by surrounding ourselves with people who
keep us grounded.

We prepare by choosing hope,
even under heavy skies.

We prepare by remembering our own strength,
the kind we didn't know we had until we needed it.

And we prepare by trusting that:
Even when the winds pick up,
the rain comes down hard,
and everything feels uncertain...
You are not alone.

Even the storm passing through the Nook carries
inspiration that ...*You're still standing.*

Reflection Part III

This section was about rooting deeper, trusting what's ahead, and preparing for what's next.

Maybe you've weathered a storm.
Maybe you're holding onto your "Plan B."
Maybe you're just trying to feel seen in a season of change.

Now that you've read these stories, take a gentle breath and reflect:

- **What part of your journey needs protecting right now?**

- **What part of your heart is quietly preparing for something new?**

- **Where can you soften the pressure and still stay grounded?**

Let the answers come without force.
Let the clarity arrive when it's ready.

Keep protecting what matters.
Keep preparing for what's possible.
You're doing it.

Part IV:

Shine + Serve

The final section of this book
is a soft exhale and a steady inhale.

It's about rising from what you've walked through,
and rooting into who you're becoming.
Let's finish this together.
Rooted. Rising. Ready.

34. Do Life Like No One Is Watching

Good morning from the Nook!

It's been a minute since I got to grab my coffee,
my camera, and my calm...
and step into this little slice of morning peace.

The birds are singing their usual chorus.
And even though the sun's not shining today,
it's still a beautiful start.

You ever notice how you can smell the flowers more
intensely right before it rains?

It's like the world exhales,
and I find myself breathing deeper just to take it all in.

This is perfect deer-watching weather.

It's like they come out right before a storm,
sensing that fewer eyes are on them.

Like maybe they're thinking,
"Who would be out here now?"

Well… me!

And even though they're timid,
they still do their thing.

They graze, explore,
and move with their own rhythm,
like no one's watching.

They live like no one's watching.

And honestly…
That might be the exact reminder I needed.

To live more freely.
To show up fully.
To keep doing the thing, even if no one claps.
Even if no one sees.

Because when you live like no one's watching,
that's when your truest self shows up.

Proof that when you stop performing and just live,
Life is beautiful.

35. Root for Her. Rise with Her.

Good morning from the Nook!

Today, I'm inspired by YOU.

Yes, to all the women reading this.
The women running households,
side gigs, full-time jobs
and doing it all with purpose.

Some of you are growing businesses.
Some of you are raising babies,
or starting new chapters.

Some of you are holding it all together,
when no one even knows what you're carrying.

And still...**you show up.**
You cheer for others.
You post about your friend's business.

You place the order,
share the link,
drop the comment,
and say, "I see you."

That kind of support matters.
It builds more than just momentum,
it builds belief.

And for those of us building something from scratch,
your presence,
your purchase,
your pep talk,
It's everything.

There is more than enough room for all of us.

So if you've got a business, small, big,
 or barely blooming,
Share it.
Talk about it.
Let others know what you're building.

You never know who's watching,
who's been praying for exactly what you offer.

And if you're not building something right now,
Support someone who is.

Root for her.
Rise with her.

Because that's how we all grow.

36. A New Chapter Is Calling

Good morning from the Nook!

A few days ago, I shared what might be my favorite
animal photo I've ever taken,
a praying mantis,
wide-eyed and staring straight at me.

This morning? Two more.
Smaller. Not quite as photogenic.

But still... right there.
Waiting.
Three in two days?
I couldn't help myself...I Googled it.

One meaning said:
"Take time to think deeply about your life
and your next steps."

Oh yes...that speaks to me.

Another said:
"To embody spirit and passion."

The Nook has always been my space to pause.

To think. To create.
To be inspired and to inspire.

To reflect. To reset. To dream.

And what I'm taking from these tiny visitors is this:
It's okay to slow down.
It's okay to regroup.
It's okay to not have the next thing fully mapped.

Life looks different than it did six months ago.
Even three months ago.

So maybe...this is a clean slate.
A new chapter already in motion.

A quieter kind of courage rising.

Stillness may not be my strong suit,
but progress?
I'm getting pretty good at that.

37. Grow With the Flow

Good morning from the Nook!

After grabbing my coffee and camera
settling into my favorite spot,
And that' when I heard them.

Who?
Owls.
Actually... two, I think.
I've not seen them, but they were close.

So as I'm reaching for my camera,
on the little table next to me is a tin pot
where I planted lavender
 (a solid mosquito strategy, by the way).

But I took a closer look,
something else is growing.

Tiny plants I didn't plant.
They found a way to grow anyway.
But how.

How did they get there?

They were carried by the wind.

They left the space they started in,
not because they wanted to,
but because they had to.

There was no more room to grow where they were.

So they trusted...
That the wind would lift them
The soil would welcome them.

And if given the chance,
they would grow again.

And I realized... that's what I'm doing too.

Sometimes, you have to leave the place where you
stopped growing.

Even when it's familiar.
Even when it's hard.

You have to trust that,
even if you don't know where you'll land,
Faith will carry you.

And you will rise again.

With Chris's love and support,
I've made the decision to leave
a space where I wasn't growing ,
and step into one where I believe I will.

My faith reminds me:

> *I don't have to have it all figured out.*
> *I just have to trust the wind.*
> *Grow with the flow.*

38. Don't Dim the Spark
That Lit You

Good morning from the Nook!

While I do love pulling inspiration
from my favorite morning spot,
this morning's message comes from somewhere else.

I'm looking at all you amazing women out there.
Running a business.
Running a household.
Working a full-time job (or two).

And still finding the energy to show up,
with love, passion, and purpose.

Friends near and far,
women I know personally
and women I've never met.

You're out there being the
FabYOUlous go-getters you are.

And yes, there's a lot of life to juggle.
But when you find your passion,
something that just lights you up inside...

There's room for all of us.
You don't have to compete to be seen.
You don't have to be loud to be valuable.
You just have to be you and show up.

And for those of you who support me,
whether it's sharing a post,
leaving a kind comment,
I see you.
I'm so grateful for you.

Because here's the magic we often forget:
Someone is always watching.
Not in a pressure-filled way,
but in a hope-filled one.

They're watching to find courage,
to feel less alone,
because they need exactly what you offer.

So keep showing up.

There's more than enough room for your light.

39. Don't Give Up

Good morning from the Nook!

In true Autumn fashion, I imagined waking up,
throwing on a cozy sweater,
and stepping into the Nook,
with both hands wrapped around a
steaming cup of coffee,
like I needed protection from the chill.

Yeah... no.
It's already 80 degrees.
So none of that happened.

But this did:
As I walked out the door,
a very large grasshopper parachuted
from the light fixture straight into the Hostas.

Then I noticed another little guy
perched on a Hosta leaf.
And a squirrel was rustling nearby.

Here's the thing,
I thought the Hostas were done for the season.

Their flowers were gone.
No birds, bees, or butterflies had come around lately.
The leaves aren't lush and green anymore.
They've faded.

But this morning...
The Hostas reminded me,
they still had something to offer.

Despite their fading appearance,
they're still providing.
Shelter. Rest. Safety.
A place for creatures I didn't even notice at first.

And I thought to myself...
How could I pull something that's still giving?

So here's what the Nook whispered today:

- *Don't give up when you're feeling down.*

- *Don't give up when you don't look your best.*

- *Don't give up when the world stops showing up to admire you.*

- *Don't give up when others think you should.*

Because you might still be giving,
in ways you don't even realize.

You're still needed.

You still matter.

There's still something left inside you,
even if it looks different than before.

Just don't give up.

41. Grow Anyway

Good morning from the Nook!

Sitting here with my coffee,
enjoy the sounds of the day getting started,
I couldn't help but notice
this little plant growing out of an old pot.

By all logic, it shouldn't be thriving.
The pot is tucked under the Nook roof.
No sunlight hits it directly.

And unless its human (aka me) remembers to water it,
it gets nothing.

There used to be a vibrant lily growing here.
But that's long gone now.

So... why this new little leaf?
Why now?
How?

There's no fresh soil.
No steady watering routine.
No real attention paid to it.
And yet ...there it is.

Planted.
Centered.
Proud.
Growing anyway.

And that's when it hit me:
There's inspiration all around us,
we just need to *notice it.*

That little plant didn't wait for perfect conditions.
It didn't ask for approval.
It didn't check the forecast.
It just believed in its ability to grow.

It's a tiny, leafy reminder:
Be stubborn with your goals.
Be flexible with your methods.

And above all ...believe in your ability to rise.

Even when everything around you whispers,
"You can't"...
Grow anyway.

41. Your Sunshine

Good morning from the Nook!

Stepping into this surprisingly cool June morning,
pistachio muffin in hand.

The birds are already in full harmony mode.

It's like the sun is the Nook's alarm clock.
I swear those Hosta sprigs weren't standing
that tall before the light hit them.

There's just something about the sun.
It changes everything.

It lifts moods.
It brings clarity.
It warms.
It helps things grow.

But here's the other side...
The sun can burn, too.
So we prepare. We protect. We notice.

And that got me thinking,
we chase "sunshine" in so many ways,
for validation, recognition and
motivation from the outside.

But remember...
You might crave the warmth, but don't let it scorch you.
You might look to the light, but your real growth starts
within.
You might want clarity, but don't let someone else's light
blind your path.

And while you might seek the sun, never forget:
You can shine without it.
You don't need someone else to make you glow.
You don't need perfect conditions to rise.

So protect your joy.
Honor your energy.
And never — ever — let anyone steal your sunshine.
Now go soak in the day.

And if you're anything like me? SPF 100, always.

42. A Little Help is Huge

Good morning from the Nook!

It's a foggy, morning as I step into my favorite spot.
The birds are singing.
Tree frogs are chiming in,
giving a little help.

And just as I settle into my chair,
the red-tailed hawk swoops by with
a solo squawk of her own,
giving a little help.

It's not the lush season yet.
The flowers haven't arrived.

The Hosta leaves haven't stretched tall.
The bees aren't buzzing through the blooms.
But I know it's coming.

So what does inspiration look like on a foggy, gray
morning?

As I brushed away brittle leaves,
placed my coffee on the table,
the Nook whispered something small,
but powerful:

It always gives a little help.
You just have to trust in its timing and
have faith.

I get to share something I love,
Pouring into others.
Showing up, to give a little help.

Backing someone else's melody
with a little harmony of my own.

Because just like the tree frogs
supporting the songbirds.

Your voice matters,
even when it's not the loudest.

And that's the reminder:
Whether you're offering help or receiving it,

A little help is huge.

Sometimes it's a kind word.
Sometimes it's presence.
Sometimes it's just showing up and saying,
"I'm here."

There are so many ways to help.

And no matter how strong we are,
we all need a little support, sometimes.

You never know how much your help might mean to
someone else.

43. We Still Get to Choose Light

Good morning from the Nook!

I haven't been able to enjoy this space
the past few weekends,
too much rain.

But today? I'm back.
The air is cooler.
The sun isn't as strong.

And the crunch of fallen leaves underfoot reminds me
that a lot has changed since my last visit.

But no matter what's different,
no matter how uncertain life feels,
I will always look for the good.
I will always reach for the light.

Because I must.

It's easy to be pulled under by negativity.
Easy to stay stuck in the what-ifs.
Easy to shrink in seasons of waiting.
But not today.

This week lit a spark.
A new fire.

A reminder that even in the unknown,
purpose still calls.

I've found a way to keep helping others.
To keep serving with heart.
To pair passion with possibility.

And with the support of my favorite person, Chris,
I know we'll walk into whatever's next together.

Life has a way of switching paths,
but we'll face it,
side by side,
step by step.

It's our journey,
but ultimately, it's His plan.
So today, I'm choosing light.

I'm choosing hope.
I'm choosing the brighter thought.
And if you ever need some of that light sprinkled your
way...
You know where to find me.

Epilogue

Serving Others

Life has been full lately, full of work, full of growth, full of movement. And I'm so grateful for every bit of busy.

But I recently saw a post that made me pause. It said something like: "*If you're waiting for God -serve.*" And it got me thinking: Am I serving enough?

There are so many ways to serve, family, friends, strangers, your community, even your calling. And your list might look different than mine. That's okay.

Sometimes I wonder: Where do I find time to serve? And then I look at the Hosta garden, the heart of the Nook. It shelters birds and bees, bunnies and butterflies. Even wilted, it still gives. Even when fading, it serves. When it's tired, it rests. When it returns, it blooms.

So maybe it's not about doing more. Maybe it's about serving with what you have — fully and faithfully — then resting. Like the Hosta: Give what you've got. Then rest. And when you return, come back ready to serve again.

Reflection Part IV

This section was about standing tall in your truth,
even when your path shifts,
your pace slows, or your view gets foggy.

Maybe you've outgrown a space.
Maybe you're being planted somewhere new.
Maybe you're finally seeing how far you've come.

Whatever your season...
You're allowed to rest.
You're allowed to reroute.
You're allowed to rise, gently and fully, in your own rhythm.

Let this space hold your thoughts.
Let it honor your process.
Let it remind you.

Your roots are deep enough.
Your growth is already happening.
Your next step is yours to take.

Nook Reflections

- Where in your life are you learning to slow down?

- What soft truth are you holding onto right now?

- What's something you're no longer rushing?

- How does stillness feel to you today?

You're not behind. You're blooming in your own rhythm.

Quiet Space to Reflect

There's no wrong way to grow.

Nook Reflections

What are you still carrying that no longer holds you?

 *Even slow growth is still growth.*

Let It Out, Then Let It Go

You're allowed to write the hard parts too.
What's been heavy on your heart?"

Soft Vision Board (In Words)

"What do you want the next season of your
life to feel like? List words, moods, dreams ...no filter."

The Circle Reflection

"Who's been in your corner lately?

Write a gratitude note to someone
(even if they never see it)."

The Letting Go List

"What are you ready to release?
Write it. Bless it. Leave it behind."

Letter to Future You

"Write to the version of you who will read this again in one year. What do you want her to remember?"

_____/_____/_____

Dear Future Me,

Be safe   Be healthy   Be kind

www.ingramcontent.com/pod-product-compliance
Lightning Source LLC
Chambersburg PA
CBHW051631120626
46551CB00014B/2033